Obsessive

Compulsive

Disorder

Obsessive Compulsive Disorder
A Survival Guide for Family and Friends

By Roy C.

Obsessive Compulsive Anonymous World Services, Inc.
New Hyde Park, New York

Publisher's note:
This book is based on personal experience. Its contents are *not* intended to replace professional help which should be sought from a competent doctor. A full list of resources can be found in the back of this book.

ISBN: 0-9628066-1-7
Library of Congress Catalog Number: 93-83800

03
7 6 5 4

Manufactured in the United States of America

Cover Design: Chuck Abrams

Illustrator: Mike Reed

Editor: Shannon Rothenberger

Contents

Introduction

Obsessive Compulsive Disorder (OCD) can be a difficult illness for *everyone* involved. The purpose of this book is to help the families and friends of those with OCD. For the purposes of this book we refer to these people as Person/People with OCD or PWOCD to make it clear that they are people, and not a disease or a problem. OCD is a chronic illness like cancer, chemical addiction or clinical depression in that it is often progressive and usually not curable, but it *is* treatable, and with treatment people with OCD can live full, healthy lives.

You might be thinking right now: "I'm not the one who needs help! It's my son (or my wife or my father) who needs help. *I* don't have OCD!" True, but you are probably also suffering as a result. A family in which one of the members has a chronic illness is a family under stress. If you are paging through this book, it means you are probably concerned about a loved one with OCD. His or her OCD symptoms have likely placed you in an occasional or constant caregiver role that is very demanding and is taking its toll on you. You may not even realize how much stress you are under as family crises put all the attention on the family member who seems to be in the "most" trouble. Like many of us were, you are probably accustomed to *not thinking about yourself* very much. It may seem selfish or unnecessary, or you may feel you don't have the time to take some of your focus off the PWOCD and take time for yourself. If there is only one message this book carries to you, we hope it is that *taking care of yourself* will improve your relationship with the PWOCD. In this family manual we offer you the hope that *you* can live a happy, full life even if your loved one *doesn't* fully recover from OCD. We will also give you some suggestions for what you can do for the PWOCD without hurting yourself. We hope this book makes your life a little easier and your relationship more rewarding.

What is Obsessive Compulsive Disorder?

*Obsessive Compulsive Disorder (or Obsessive Compulsive Neurosis). The essential feature of this disorder is recurrent obsessions or compulsions sufficiently severe to cause marked distress, be time consuming, or sufficiently interfere with the person's normal routine, occupational functioning, or usual social activities or relationships with others.

Obsessions are persistent ideas, thoughts, impulses, or images that are experienced, at least initially, as intrusive and senseless — for example a parent having repeated impulses to kill a loved child, or a religious person having recurrent blasphemous thoughts. The person attempts to ignore or suppress such thoughts or impulses or to neutralize them with some other thought or action. The person recognizes that the obsessions are the products of his or her own mind, and are not imposed from without (as in the delusion of thought insertion).

The most common obsessions are repetitive thoughts of violence (e.g., killing one's child), contamination (e.g., becoming infected by shaking hands), and doubt (e.g., repeatedly wondering whether one has performed some act, such as having hurt someone in a traffic accident).

Compulsions are repetitive, purposeful and intentional behaviors that are performed in response to an obsession, according to certain rules, or in a stereotyped fashion. The behavior is designed to neutralize or to prevent discomfort or some dreaded event or situation. However, either the activity is not connected in a realistic way with what it is designed to neutralize or prevent, or it is

*Reprinted with permission from *The Diagnostic and Statistical Manual of Mental Disorders, Third Edition, Revised.* Copyright 1987 American Psychiatric Association.

clearly excessive. The act is performed with a sense of subjective compulsion that is coupled with a desire to resist the compulsion (at least initially). The person recognizes that his or her behavior is excessive or unreasonable (this may not be true for young children and may no longer be true for people whose obsessions have evolved into overvalued ideas) and does not derive pleasure from carrying out the activity, although it provides a release of tension. The most common compulsions involve hand-washing, counting, checking and touching.

When the person attempts to resist a compulsion, there is a sense of mounting tension that can be immediately relieved by yielding to the compulsion. In the course of the illness, after repeated failure at resisting the compulsions, the person may give in to them and no longer experience a desire to resist them.

Associated features. Depression and anxiety are common. Frequently there is a phobic avoidance of situations that involve the content of the obsessions, such as dirt or contamination. For example, a person with obsessions about dirt may avoid public restrooms; a person with obsessions about contamination may avoid shaking hands with strangers.

Age at onset. Although the disorder usually begins in adolescence or early adulthood, it may begin in childhood.

Course. The course is usually chronic, with waxing and waning of symptoms.

Impairment. Impairment is often moderate or severe. In some cases acting according to compulsions may become the major life activity.

Complications. Complications include Major Depression and the abuse of alcohol and anxiolytics.

Predisposing factors. No information.

Prevalence. Although the disorder was previously thought to be relatively rare in the general population, recent community

2

studies indicate that mild forms of the disorder may be relatively common.

Sex ratio. This disorder is equally common in males and in females.

Western Suffolk Psychological Services
755 New York Avenue - Suite 200
Huntington, New York 11743

I would like to take this opportunity to note that this excellent "Survival Guide" deals with a group mostly neglected by all the other existing OCD writings. Until now, the identified patient has always been the main focal point. I have always believed that when an individual suffers from OCD, the potential exists for family and friends to suffer as well.

Groups such as OCA, and principles such as those embodied in this book help these 'significant others' to refocus on the bottom-line issue of responsibility. More specifically, I mean the answers to questions such as - "Who is responsible for the sufferer's illness?", "Who is responsible for managing the sufferer's symptoms and recovery?", and finally, "Who is responsible for each individual's life and happiness?". A clear understanding of the answers to these questions by sufferers and those close to them, can lead to a recovery of everyone's life. A confusion can only lead to continuing and prolonged disturbance for all.

For families and friends coping with someone's OCD, there are few reliable road maps. The disorder creates paradoxical situations where intuition often leads everyone in an opposite direction, and away from the desired result. Those surrounding the patient are led to help when they should step away, and conversely, to pull back from where they can be truly helpful. They can erect extra obstacles as they try to make things 'easier', or sweep obstacles away as they do things which at first may strike them as being too 'tough'.

5

As someone who treats both patients and those close to them, I welcome this, and any book which can shed light on these issues. Professionals, too, can benefit from increasing their understanding.

Based upon this, and your previous book, it is clear that you are doing something quite special and important.

With all encouragement,

Fred Penzel, Ph.D.

Obsessive-compulsive disorder causes severe distress both for the individuals suffering from it and for the members of these individuals' families. Parents of the patients feel guilty and responsible for the problem, and other family members are pushed into participating in compulsive rituals. OCD also wreaks havoc with the sexual relationship between OCD sufferers and their spouses.

I recently read the draft for this family survival guide, and I found the suggestions and advice contained in it to be extremely helpful. The guide integrates techniques from behavior therapy with the *detachment* approach of Al-Anon, and I think this combination is well worth trying by families coping with OCD.

Douglas R. Hogan, Ph.D.

Clinical Psychologist

Garden City, N.Y.

June 21, 1993

NORTH RALEIGH PSYCHIATRY &
ADDICTION MEDICINE, P.A.
920-A PAVERSTONE DRIVE
RALEIGH, NORTH CAROLINA   27615

February 8, 1993

Many thanks for letting me know about the upcoming book for relatives and families of people with Obsessive Compulsive Disorder. I have felt for a long time that such a book was very much needed. We have so many excellent books for relatives of patients with illnesses such as dementia or schizophrenia. There has been a great hiatus as far as families with an OCD member. The idea of a support group similar to Al-Anon would serve to fill a tremendous need that I have encountered over the years in working with patients with OCD and their families. It is very frequently as you might expect that I encounter problems with families in which they are very much in need of help as to what behavior might be enabling behavior such as we see in alcoholic families and families with drug addiction and what would be realistic positive and appropriate behavior all in the part of the family. This can be a particularly difficult problem in OCD families. I am really delighted about your undertaking and you have my full support.

With kindest regards, I remain

Sincerely yours,

Wilmer C. Betts, M.D.

WCB/mwn

Doing The Right Thing

To the family,

Reflecting back on my own experience with my obsessive compulsive family member, of course, as a psychologist, I would say it's imperative to remain emotionally detached from any pain that you cause (in the course of following a program of recovery). In the early days of medicine, doctors may have seemed extremely callous and emotionally detached when they operated without the benefit of anesthesia. When dealing with this disorder you too might appear to be callous and indifferent, especially toward loved ones.

Our compassion for our loved ones could be the very thing that prolongs the illness. It's not unlike families which enable alcoholics; by fixing the problems they, themselves, become the problem. I think, at first, it's natural to be overly compassionate.

The dilemma for family members is trying to figure out the rightness of our actions. There were far too many days when I just didn't know what was right; there were so many conflicting opinions. I finally realized that, because it was one of my children, I was trying to be perfect and I had to have perfect solutions. I was constantly trying to fix reality.

There was nothing wrong with my child; it was my *view* that something was wrong. My child was perfect — I just had to change my view. I finally realized that it was my own stuff that was complicating our world.

I think I was stuck feeling responsible, feeling ashamed. Now I have complete acceptance of myself and my children and I wouldn't have them

11

any other way. As a result, all our lives got better.

My heart is pure within and yours is too. There comes a time when we have to trust ourselves to do the right thing. We go within to the natural laws that guide us and when we go outside, we ask a loving God to guide us. Don't get stuck in putting other people's ideas and opinions above yours, no matter who they are. Stay with your heart.

"It's only with the heart that one can rightly see because everything that's essential is invisible to the eye."

Today I'm emotionally detached from any disorder of my children but *not from them*. I believe that we all strive to share our vulnerabilities without judgment. Some of our problems have actually created a sense of connectedness since we attempted to resolve our problems in an acceptable manner. Our intimate feelings were born out of conflict and knowing we were there for each other, no matter what. So, no matter how I say it, doing the right thing is always coming from the heart.

Janet Greeson, Ph.D.

Your Life Matters, A consulting service for matters of the Heart.

800-515-1995

Living With and Loving Someone Who Has OCD

Many have lived long enough with an OCD sufferer to know what doesn't help. We each feel at times that we want to rescue, cure and protect the person from their OCD. We have wanted them to realize how much the illness is hurting everyone and we have tried everything to get them to stop. Sometimes, out of anger and frustration, we have yelled, "Just Stop!" And then there are times when it seemed easier and faster just to do the compulsion *for* them: "Let me check (clean, count) it for you." We hoped this would reassure the person or make him see how nonsensical the behavior is, but we just ended up getting caught up in the disease itself, which is very draining!

It is natural to try to make routines easier to reduce tension and delay for the family, but it only *seems* "easier for everyone" if you close windows for someone who is paralyzed by fear of them being open or if you pay all the bills yourself so the PWOCD won't recount and obsess about doing it right. Many of us have even gone to extremes such as washing our clean clothes or ourselves for the PWOCD who continually insists we're contaminated.

Anger is a normal emotional reaction to the confusing, time-stealing nature of OCD and it is common to scream at and threaten a PWOCD. Many of us did not carry out our threats such as to leave, pull out financially or punish them in some way. Logical arguments about why the OCD behavior and fears are irrational don't work either. Nor do tearful scenes expressing the loss of your healthy relationship and happy homelife (though feelings of sadness about what OCD has taken from you are perfectly natural). Bribes are equally ineffective, though they are often tried by those of us desperate for a solution. Buying things for the PWOCD if he doesn't display any symptoms for a certain period of time doesn't work. Rewards are equally as useless as all of the previously mentioned responses to OCD behavior. As a matter of fact, these behaviors often make the OCD worse.

What *does* work is to first learn about the illness of OCD. Things happen to you, but you also happen to them. As you learn about the illness, try to separate it from the person and how you feel about him or her. Later on, we will discuss family dynamics and you can explore your role in the family. The more insight you have, the less you will feel victimized by the OCD. Read as much as you can about OCD and do not be afraid to ask your doctor questions and get second, third or as many opinions as you need on treatments. Be assertive when dealing with doctors. Don't just be a "good patient" and follow orders silently. There are many new medications for OCD and you want to make sure you have a doctor who is communicating honestly with you and sensitive to the patient's needs and possible side effects of medication. Don't blame and attack the doctor. Do make sure you are being heard.

Search until you find a qualified therapist with whom you feel comfortable. Work closely with that person to develop an understanding of your loved one's particular symptoms of OCD, what recovery you can reasonably expect and the tools for living and changing with the illness.

What sort of tools are we talking about? You won't find them in a hardware store. They are concepts, attitudes and behaviors that we recommend to help you to deal with OCD and your loved one who has it. Our goal is acceptance. Accepting the OCD doesn't mean giving up and becoming passive. The acceptance we experience comes from a process of learning about OCD, experiencing and expressing feelings, taking action, making choices, getting our needs met and letting go of unrealistic expectations for the PWOCD and perfectionistic standards for ourselves. You can do it too, and we believe that when you practice these skills you will feel a growing serenity and inner strength and that life, one day at a time with the PWOCD, can become manageable. That is what we mean by acceptance.

The Al-Anon family program, which developed in response and relation to alcoholism, is a useful model for regaining sanity and finding joy and personal growth when you love someone who has OCD, whether they are willing to work on recovery or not. Three simple Al-Anon principles are applicable to living with a PWOCD and they are essential to surviving the situation:

> Your family didn't cause OCD.

> Your family can't control OCD.

> Your family can't cure OCD. [1.]

These ideas may seem radical to you, or even ridiculous, because they may challenge what can be years of beliefs you have about the PWOCD and their behavior. It is normal to try to analyze the possible causes of the behavior, which unfortunately often leads to blaming someone for it, or having a feeling of being blamed, even by yourself. Analyzing the cause or assigning blame does not help the situation and creates an unhealthy climate in the family; people divide into predictable reactive coping roles, which we will explore later on. These roles are painful and create isolation and conflict.

For now, try to put aside questions beginning with "Why...?", such as "Why OCD?", "Why her?", "Why me?" and "Why *our* family?" "Why...?" questions do not have answers in relation to chronic illnesses, however poetically they may be expressed in the *Book of Job*.

But you want answers. Of course you want answers; we are all desperate for them in the crisis situation that is OCD. The OCD symptoms and the conflicts around them appear baffling and unsolvable. The most useful answers, however, the ones that *actually work*, answer questions beginning with "How...?"

"How can I help the person with OCD?"

There is a lot of help you can give by *stopping* some of the things you may be doing. Family and friends can try *not* to engage in rituals that the sufferer feels compelled to perform. Family and

15

friends can refrain from answering obsessive questions such as "Did I hurt you when I kissed you?" or "Did I count the change right?" Answering those questions and participating in OCD rituals are what Al-Anon defines as "enabling" the behavior.

Enabling is when you protect someone from the consequences of their actions, depriving them of the right to learn and grow. Enabling says, "You are not competent. I am in control here," and the PWOCD gets the message that they are dependent on you, which is humiliating for them and draining for you. Enabling encourages a dependent strategy by the PWOCD for protection and to get attention. Dependent people become insecure about their abilities, and fearful of change, failure and independence. Worst of all, enabling actually encourages the illness to manifest and grow. It feeds the disease like bellows fan a fire.

How do you stop enabling? What are you supposed to do when these situations come up? The Al-Anon suggestion is to "detach, with love." [2.] "Detaching" sounds like a cold, uncaring reaction at first, but it is very different from not caring. Detaching with love means you detach emotionally from the person's *behavior*, without rejecting the person. You don't have to react to everything people do. Detaching is difficult to do at first because the dependent person's genuine fear and pain feels like it "pulls you in." Often the PWOCD doesn't want a solution; he wants the attention.

If you find it difficult to break this spell, you could be enabling because of low self esteem. If you only feel worthwhile when you are needed, you need to work on ignoring negative feelings about yourself and giving up perfectionist standards. Therapy and support groups can help you identify the sources of negative feelings about yourself and you can start to notice and appreciate your good qualities. Some ideas for taking care of yourself, which we will cover later on, can help you increase your self esteem.

Another skill to help you stop enabling the PWOCD involves the creation of boundaries, which are not walls between people, but ways to allow each of you your freedom. A person with good boundaries knows he or she is not responsible for someone else's feelings or behavior. Your emotional state is not dictated by the feelings of others and it is not your fault if the PWOCD is exhibiting symptoms today. The skill of detaching with love is a profound and powerful response, but it is not developed overnight. Each person and situation is unique and everyone learns new behaviors on his own timetable. Try not to expect perfection from yourself, and most important, do not judge yourself harshly for your feelings and abilities, past or present. Remember: You did the best you could and you are doing the best you can.

Do not give someone else's illness power over the way you feel about yourself. Do not make the OCD more important than it already is.

How to deal with obsessive questions:

1. Don't answer them. If your loved one is in the car with you and he wants to know if he just "ran someone over," let him know that you don't answer obsessive questions. The PWOCD knows deep down that he is just obsessing anyway.

2. "Flood" the obsessions with the worst case scenario. If the PWOCD is obsessing about having left the oven on, exaggerate the consequences. With love and humor let the PWOCD know that if he doesn't check the oven again, the house will surely burn down! This lets everyone see the obsession in a more realistic light.

How not to take over their responsibilities:

— No excuses to the boss if she is late.

— No notes to the baseball coach saying he was sick when he was ritualizing. He *is* sick with OCD but it isn't our job to make excuses for him.

— Don't finish rituals for the PWOCD.

— DO love the person, but don't get caught up in the illness.

17

— Expect small gains early on and reinforce these improvements. Let the PWOCD know you're on his side.

Behavior Therapy

With the help of a behavior therapist, you can encourage the PWOCD to face their fears and refrain from performing the rituals. Over time, sometimes quickly, sometimes gradually, repeated success or lack of dire outcomes convinces a PWOCD that it's okay to feel the fear but to "do it" or "not do it" *anyway*, whatever the desired behavior may be.

For example, a person with contamination fears can use a public restroom and not have to shower afterward. The fears of contamination pass with repeated exposure without compensating rituals.

Of course, it is not necessary or possible to *force* anyone to modify his behavior. If attempts at behavior change are creating too many arguments or meeting with strong resistance, leave the treatment up to the therapist and detach from the results. Don't tell the PWOCD how disappointed you are. Support her by letting her know you are there for *her*, but not the illness. It helps not to overdiscuss the OCD symptoms, as you'll find yourself repeating futile reassurances time and time again.

After all, the object is to regain or discover a lost or yet-to-be-lived relationship with the person, a relationship full of all the warmth, intimacy, comfort and surprises you both deserve.

Medications

Medications are a popular topic for PWOCD and their loved ones. There are medications available from psychiatrists specifically for OCD. Some people have been helped dramatically. The PWOCD needs to see a psychiatrist to discuss medication options that might be available for him.

Medications can be a source of changes for both of you as you wait for them to work and deal with possible side effects. There may also be strains on your finances or extra work filling out insurance forms to pay for prescriptions and medical bills. As a family member, you may also be swamped with calls from friends and relatives, depending on how many people you have told — another important issue that requires communication between the PWOCD and his family — disclosure! (You may need to create a compromise between the PWOCD's desire for privacy and your desire for support.) People want to know the current condition of the PWOCD or if the latest medication is working and this can be exhausting for you. One thing you can do is ask the PWOCD to answer those calls, as they are about him, anyway. That way the PWOCD can give or withhold information at his own discretion, eliminating a major potential source of conflict in the family. You can also ask other family members or friends to help you with this task, as well as the enormous volume of paperwork that medical treatments can produce.

Obsessive Compulsive Anonymous (OCA)

The Twelve-Step program of OCA has helped many PWOCD to recover from OCD. Group meetings can help break the isolation experienced by the PWOCD. The sense of shame and secrecy of being "the only one" is eliminated. OCA also has many specific suggestions for the PWOCD to help break the cycle of OCD and return to a normal life. OCA is a Twelve-Step program which guides its members to surrender to a spiritual source of their own choosing in order to change. The Twelve Steps are also a method for discovering and addressing unhealthy character traits which PWOCD often share.

As a person who loves someone with OCD, you want to bring this help to her and you want her to use this information immediately and without reserve. You may be surprised to find the PWOCD reluctant to try any treatment despite her obvious suffering.

It could be that the PWOCD is:

— afraid of treatment

— doubts it will work for him

— is in denial about the severity of the problem

— is fearful of the treatment actually working

"To say I have a disease of sorts is really comforting, in a way, if I could be cured. But I don't know what this would look like and I can't really imagine it. I am so used to feeling badly about myself that it actually feels somewhat sinful to TRY to feel better." — OCA member [3.]

The reasons some people are afraid of recovery are that there can be secondary gains from having OCD and he or she might be afraid to lose these perks:

— not having to work, or working minimally

— few responsibilities

— protection from the outside world and his or her own feelings.

OCD acts as a smokescreen for painful feelings; it provides distraction from having to feel emotions which are feared as undesirable or unmanageable. The illness also serves as a painful barrier to addressing real life issues such as a painful childhood, the inability to succeed in business or poor relationships.

Current theory has it that OCD originates as a result of a predisposition for the illness with a resultant biochemical imbalance in the brain. This does not mean that a PWOCD has to be a passive victim of OCD, though some may use OCD as a reason not to change or take risks, including treatment. *While the PWOCD is not at fault for his or her illness, he or she is still responsible for working on recovery!* It is not as important for the PWOCD to dwell on what caused the illness, but to focus on what he or she can do about it!

"There's a lot of talk about OCD being caused by a chemical imbalance in the brain. My personal theory about this is that it is possibly a chemical imbalance, but I believe that we trip the chemicals off with our emotions and our reactions. I believe that people with OCD hold on to resentments much more than the 'average, normal person.' People with OCD are more sensitive than other people, but in practicing the Twelve Steps, a person can come to like this more peaceful way of life." — OCA Member [4.]

Denial

Often the sufferer will deny the severity of his or her illness. He may insist that the OCD is bothering others more than it bothers him. Usually, though, the PWOCD is acutely aware of his inner pain and turmoil. Denial serves to put life in a holding pattern. Since procrastination is also a trait among Obsessive-Compulsives, this double bind of denial and procrastination can hinder them from taking any steps toward recovery.

The Twelve-Step program of OCA especially helps the PWOCD break through his or her denial. The PWOCD identifies with others and sees herself in others. Guilt and shame surrounding OCD subside and finally the PWOCD can realize the true severity of her illness. Another benefit is when the newcomer to OCA sees others getting well, she realizes that she too can recover if she takes the necessary actions. OCA reinforces the idea that the OCD will not go away be itself — action is required for recovery.

As with any recovery work — Easy Does It! This slogan (which evolved in Alcoholics Anonymous) means: Don't try to solve all the problems created by OCD at once. Less action is more — less involvement with others' behavior equals less frustration for you. Set your own pace and tackle problems one at a time, as you are ready.

21

Family Dynamics

Years spent with OCD take their toll on families. Simply living with OCD rituals can be challenging. Each family member develops a style of coping with the illness to reduce tension and try to manage the situation because it makes them feel afraid. These styles are called roles and while some roles may be useful and people may play different roles interchangeably, it is dangerous to get trapped in a family role. Roles, as defined by the program for Adult Children of Alcoholics, limit the growth and expression of each person and create conflicts of their own. [5.]

For example, someone who takes on the role of *caretaker* will do more work than other family members and feel like a martyr. Over time this guilt-based behavior puts caretakers out of touch with themselves and their personalities can seem forced or false to others. They are prone to addictions such as overeating or compulsive shopping to numb their feelings. Children can be pressed into the roles of "little adults" and expected to help out to the point where they miss out on their childhood.

Others become *heroes* and have to succeed and accomplish constantly to compensate for family troubles. They desperately believe that if they are "good" enough and "perfect" enough, family conflicts will go away. Roles of clown (or *mascot*, according to ACOA), "invisible" person and *scapegoat* are also played by family members and there are many other possible adaptations to the crisis. *Mascots* use humor as a defense and as a result, they are usually not taken seriously.

Lost or invisible *Children* respond to crisis by disappearing and denying their feelings to the point where others are often not aware they are in the room. *Scapegoats* defuse family conflicts by acting out until it looks like *they* are the problem. They tend to become self-destructive in the process. All roles limit people's experience and harm their functioning in the world outside the family system.

Because of the gap between home reality and the ᵥ
side and the resulting troubles families of PWOCD face in the ᵥᵥ
side world, families in which illness dominates often become
isolated. There is often a sense of shame about chronic illness,
much like the shame around alcoholism. People feel stigmatized
and different from their neighbors. Secrecy about and denial of
the disease keep healing from happening and everything only gets
worse.

Poor interpersonal relations are one of the effects of OCD.
Because of the illness, the PWOCD isolates himself from his family, while at the same time, relying on them for his most basic
needs. This unbalanced situation creates an inability to form a
natural two-way give-and-take relationship with others. The situation spreads to the rest of the family as they experience the dynamics as unfair. Families of OCD gradually come to live in the
"Don't trust, don't talk, don't feel" climate of families of alcoholism or chemical addiction.

Constant blaming of the PWOCD and each other for the OCD
and the resulting strain on everyone often result in a "comfortable
misery" within the family which is very difficult to change. Both
the PWOCD and the family lock into an unhappy pattern of relating.

Surprisingly, when the PWOCD recovers, home life doesn't
automatically improve in a smooth, predictable way. The pattern
for adjustment to OCD and recovery is the same as in relation to
alcoholism, with specific stages that people experience.

"Both OCD and alcoholism are addictive, out-of-control, mis-
guided searches for feelings of relief which only result in pain."
— OCA — Recovering from OCD [6.]

The Al-Anon textbook *Al-Anon Faces Alcoholism* describes
the progression as follows: The appearance of chronic illness in a
family member disrupts healthy patterns of relating, fair divisions
of functioning, appropriate and predictable roles and realistic ex-

pectations for everyone. The pattern of this crisis begins with *Denial*.

"It is the nature of this disease that the victims do not believe they are ill." — American Medical Association definition of alcoholism (applicable to OCD). [7.]

Nor does the family want to face the possibility that something is seriously wrong with a loved one. They often justify the symptoms as normal, avoid situations where symptoms might occur, compare the sufferer to others in a way that clouds the issue, and withdraw socially for protection. In spite of all this, disorganized, apathetic and strained relationships result.

The second stage in the crisis pattern involves *Adjustment Techniques*. Roles and identities change in order to function with the OCD. Mental conflicts and personality distortions begin. Secondary crises of shame, secrecy, isolation, poor school performance, discipline problems, unemployment, loss of income, infidelity, violence and arguing can distract everyone from the OCD. A lack of clearly available community support deepens the shame and isolation for the family and an unstructured system of trial and error makes everyone feel insecure.

A realization that "This is not normal" precipitates a stage of *Attempting to Eliminate the Problem*. This is when threats, enabling and futile attempts to thwart rituals escalate. People agonize over trying to "understand" the problem and nagging becomes frequent. The PWOCD becomes the central preoccupation at home and long-term individual goals and family plans are put on hold.

This stage creates an environment of *Peak Isolation* where the problem is experienced as a part of everything and symbolic of all family conflicts. Everyone feels secretive, blamed, alienated, inadequate and abandoned. Each person's self esteem deteriorates and worry, guilt and helplessness set in as the household falls apart.

Often conditions worsen until an attitude of *"What's the use?"* dominates. In this stage the family gives up and doesn't care who knows about the problem. Respect, affection and communication among family members are replaced by tension and hostility. Random tension-relieving behaviors make people feel lost and crazy, without goals and very sad about the loss of the way they used to be.

In the next stage a solution often develops as the family *Restructures Within the Problem.* If the PWOCD was the family authority or someone who used to take a lead role can no longer cope, another family member may assume an authoritative, primary caregiving role, usually as a result of a "last straw" crisis or the removal of the PWOCD. The PWOCD is excluded, ignored, pitied, protected, given up on or given the role of "bad child," no matter how old he is. As a result of lowered expectations and new functioning, "problems" decrease and self-blame is reduced. Children feel more secure and often finances increase as other family members take jobs to help out. Nevertheless, the disease progresses.

Another solution people find at this stage is to *Escape.* They usually feel unsupported if they leave and plagued by guilt for "deserting a sick person." They may also have scapegoated themselves for the problem and think that if they leave the family will return to normal. In this strategy the *lost child* role is played, even by a spouse. The PWOCD may display more control of his or her symptoms in response to the separation, or in an attempt to get the person back. This is confusing for the family.

The final and hoped-for stage is *Recovery and Reorganization.* It may begin with a diagnosis and the start of treatment. The diagnosis of a chronic illness like OCD cay be terrifying. It is difficult to adjust to this new reality and many PWOCD and their families experience the classic response to traumatic news in stages of denial, shock, projection, anger, grief and finally, acceptance. This process is by no means quick or linear; it is more of a cycle depending on events and personalities, but the direction is toward greater acceptance and serenity.

25

In the meantime, conflicts arise from new expectations, issues of authority, doubts, distrust, old resentments and guilts. The family may have trouble with change and letting go of control. Communication can feel threatening after years of avoidance. Many caretakers of PWOCD do not want to give up their powerful roles and territories.

Common resentments burn:

— How can outsiders help my loved one when I couldn't?

— Why does *he* get all this support, but the family doesn't?

— Why do I have to cope with these changes by myself?

— The person with OCD is just being "selfish" after all *I've* done for her!

Many people in the family are not used to the PWOCD, now in recovery, exerting his freedom from the illness or making decisions. The family has grown accustomed to his depending on them. They suddenly feel unneeded. Time is the key for adjusting to these changes. It takes time to realize that the PWOCD can and needs to live his own life. In a nutshell, the family is happy about the recovery but disturbed by the change in the "balance of power" as the PWOCD flexes his new recovery muscles!

"At thirty-six finding myself suddenly turning around and saying to my husband, 'I know what I'm going to do' is very scary, especially when he doesn't suffer with OCD and he doesn't understand what I'm going through." — OCA Member [8.]

Sexual-marital relations are another common source of change which can take some courage and acceptance to handle. The partner of a PWOCD has probably gotten used to no or infrequent sex as a result of the OCD. The PWOCD previously lost interest in sex due to his or her illness. Now, in recovery the PWOCD finds sex exciting and new. Again, time will allow adjustment to this change.

As the PWOCD recovers, the family can heal too. Joint treatments with a therapist can help the family as a whole. Support groups ease change and provide basic information and human connection that heals shame and creates hope. Perspective and security are gained and goals can be set as each person learns to live in recovery.

Remember: Unless PWOCD want recovery, there are no real options for them. Needless anxiety over their condition is harmful to you. You cannot change people. If you are feeling overwhelming depression, frustration, heartbreak, anger or apathy, Al-Anon tools are an option for you. Do not enable the PWOCD *unless* it's the only way to deal with it, for instance, if the person absolutely will not be challenged.

If you feel certain the PWOCD will *not* change, and you feel as though you are losing your mind, especially in the case of a partner, parent or adult child who can be taken care of in some other way — take a risk: leave the relationship if necessary. It may be the wake-up call they need, but if not, you can save your own sanity.

If you are in a relationship with a PWOCD, remember that recovery is a process. Whether they recover or not, it is necessary for you to decide to accept their illness and live your own life, whether that means setting limits or leaving. Surrender your agenda for them to change, especially if it is unreasonable. You can't *make* someone get better. Be patient. Accept how difficult it is to have a problem with biological roots and that recovery has nothing to do with sheer will power. Do not pester the PWOCD about homework and treatments or expect improvements right away. Disconnect from the person's symptoms and let them work until they give them up. Your own compulsivity about the person's disease can run your life, but you don't have to let it.

As for results for couples, ill partners can recover and sometimes the relationship improves. And sometimes you have a chance for the first *real* relationship you've ever had with the person! Sometimes, though, the relationship falls apart. If you find

27

you need to end the relationship, let yourself do it without guilt or abandonment: *It's common for other problems within a relationship to surface as a partner recovers from a chronic illness.* These problems may be too much to resolve all at once, especially when your partner is focusing on recovering from OCD.

"I guess the painful part is when a person begins going through his or her own changes and starts to recover, it's hard for other people, whether it be friends, coworkers, acquaintances, family and especially one's spouse or significant other because the person they fell in love with is no longer the same person." — OCA Member [9.]

Whatever happens, it is not your fault. Getting well is the other person's responsibility. A point to bear in mind is that minor relapses are normal for a PWOCD. They are not to be feared. The recovery process is not a straight line, just as there are no straight lines in nature and our bodies are made up of curves. It is the overall pattern of recovery that is important — occasional slips are not preferred, but they do not signal a full relapse.

Recovery for Family Members — Taking Care of Ourselves

OCD is not a new illness, but knowledge about its treatment is new. In the past PWOCD were sometimes diagnosed as schizophrenics, depressed or generally anxious, but more commonly, their illness went undiagnosed. The treatments that work best today are medication, behavior therapy and support groups like OCA. If the PWOCD is in therapy and lives with you, his or her best chance for success will be if you work with the therapist too. Children especially need a home "co-therapist" for coaching and support. That person is usually the child's primary caregiver, though both parents and other family members can share the responsibility if they are willing. The more people at home who are educated about OCD the better!

Raising children, running a household, having a relationship with a partner and/or holding a job are enough responsibilities for most people. When you add chronic illness in the family to that equation, everything gets out of balance. OCD is intrusive and incomprehensible and suddenly there is less time for your partner or other children (the people who are not ill) and there is even less time for yourself. *All family members need emotional support and skills for living with the PWOCD.*

People with OCD feel overwhelmed by their illness and until they have some recovery, often forget about the people around them. Especially if you already come from a background where illness, addiction or general dysfunction dominated, this new family crisis can easily recreate that formative situation for you and your role of "over-helper" is waiting, like a suit that still fits.

That is why it is essential to find a therapist who will also talk with you about *yourself*, not just the PWOCD. A therapist can help

29

you set boundaries: decide what helpers do and what the patient can do for herself. You can ask your therapist to help you set time limits per day for your involvement with the person's OCD. Sometimes it takes an objective, outside view to determine what is excessive.

The family-systems point of view in therapy is relatively new, so if you find counselors who are experienced in this method, work with them! It's worth it. A great relief for you will be if the therapist can act as a mediator and give other family members assignments, so all the responsibility is not on you. A therapist's trained vigilance for new symptoms and signs of recovery is shared with you as you work together.

If OCD is caught early enough in children it can be treated so that the illness does not become integrated with their personalities and they will have stronger egos.

Some therapists advise that you do *not* label a child with OCD. Their young identities are fragile and the illness can become a burdensome label, as in when a person who was told she was overweight in adolescence grows up to feel "always fat."

One seven-year-old girl suffering from OCD told her mother she thought she was crazy and wanted to die. Her fears and doubts paralyzed her and her obsessions were almost constant. In therapy, she learned that what she was having were "silly thoughts" and that her mother was not going to respond to silly thoughts. She understood that other people have "silly thoughts too" and that hers might come back from time to time, but it's okay. Her therapist also emphasized that *not every thought* is a silly one, and the child is able to distinguish by asking herself, "Is this something anyone would worry about?" Making lists of realistic worries as opposed to silly ones helped her recovery.

Two years of approach and exposure behavior techniques have helped the girl to no longer feel "crazy." Visualizing herself doing the fearful thing and being okay anyway is also working. While the mother describes her daughter (with a sense of awe and admiration) as continuing to be extremely sensitive and imaginative, by going through stressful situations, the child is learning that her fears and imaginings are much worse than the reality. She is getting better primarily through the efforts of her mother to reinforce her behavior therapy.

Such vigilance can take its toll, however. The mother of this child with OCD is beginning to attend support group meetings for family members of PWOCD to share her experience, get support and take time for herself. Many caregivers in such a situation are unaware of the stresses of caregiving, how they are affected and what kind of help is available.

A family member of a PWOCD often experiences emotional ups and downs between the confusing fears about the diagnoses to their own responses to the changing OCD symptoms, and effects on their own self esteem. There is a fine line between caring and controlling with co-dependency. Co-dependency occurs when caring becomes guilt, overresponsibility, oversacrifice and a feeling of being consumed or burnt out by someone else's illness. Co-dependency is about behaviors that don't work. These behaviors are not permanent and can be changed by working the Twelve Steps.

Though OC disorders are not commonly developed by co-dependents, most OC personalities have co-dependency issues which we share with them. Here are some character traits related to co-dependency and OCD in partner relationships:

1. We lived a "compelled role," such as rescuer, fixer and controller, coupled with fear of intimacy.

2. We were dependent: We felt threatened if our partner disagreed with us or took a step away.

3. We believed our strength and identity came from our partner. This led to possessiveness, jealousy and clinginess. In a healthy relationship, partners give each other support and caring, but our strength comes from inner and spiritual sources.

31

4. We were drama addicts: We needed tension and conflict to feed a sick excitement or comfortable misery. In a healthy relationship, we can experience a reasonable degree of stability, consistency and predictability.

5. We had a narrow focus on one person, possession or role. This led to people-pleasing: Our feelings were tied to our partners, so that if they were unhappy, we had to be sad too. They were the source of our self-esteem. Now we can each have many sources of support and identity, such as friends, business and projects.

6. We were trapped in repetition-compulsion: We re-staged our family-of-origin scenarios and power struggles. Rescuers married dependent people and ACOA's married alcoholics to try to fix the parent they could not save.

7. We battled for control. Always. Control or lack of control was central to every aspect of life.

8. We had a deep fear of abandonment. Many of us came from homes where our parents were unavailable emotionally and/or physically. Some of us entered destructive relationships if we felt they promised never feeling abandoned again.

Another indication of co-dependency is burnout. Are you burnt out? Do any of these feelings apply to you: Anxious, tired, tense, angry, lonely, used up, emotionally volatile, out of time, out of money, out of shape? If so, then you maybe are giving too much. This section of the book can show you how to give and still have something left for yourself.

The "Big Book" of Al-Anon says, "Distressed family members are often unaware of the source of their discomfort." [10.]

It goes on to list stress-related disorders which family members most often report to their doctors such as gastrointestinal problems, lower back pain, headaches, insomnia, anxiety and depression. To therapists they also complain of poor work performance and relationship troubles. In school, children may display signs of neglect, abuse, behavioral problems or truancy or they may be runaways. Even if things haven't gotten "that bad" for you, *the key symptoms for the entire family are being out of touch with feelings and the inability to trust.*

So, after we educate ourselves about the illness of OCD and the treatment for the PWOCD, it is time to learn about ourselves. If you find yourself unable to tune in to your own feelings because you are obsessing on new strategies for dealing with the PWOCD, *STOP.* Recognize that your loved one is being taken care of by a loving force greater than both of you, and that *you* are protected in the same way. If you have trouble with the spiritual side of Twelve-Step programs and feel that your loved one could have been "brain washed" into some religious cult, let it go for now. You are entitled to your beliefs, but they have not had the success for the PWOCD that you wanted, so give OCA a chance to work for them if they are willing to try it.

If the idea of a Higher Power is objectionable for you, entrust your loved one to the care of the support group or professional of their choice and step back from their process. Give the treatment a chance to work.

The Serenity Prayer (with or without the "God"):

Grant me the serenity

To accept the things I cannot change

The courage to change the things I can

And the wisdom to know the difference.

Affirming these words can give you some comfort whether you pray or not. Consider its message to learn the difference: What can and can't I change? Deep down, you already know the answers. This inner wisdom grants you confidence, patience and tolerance.

Admitting that there is a family problem is the hardest part. Once you have acknowledged a need for change, you are halfway to accomplishing it. You can begin by exploring your experience with the illness. You can share this with a therapist or support group or write it in a journal. Here are some questions to get you started:

Has your life been disrupted by someone's OCD? How?

Are you preoccupied with the OCD? How often do you think about it during the day?

Have you begun to dislike some of the things you say and do? What are some of those things? (Be specific).

Have you ever been unable to predict your own behavior because you were so worried about the PWOCD's symptoms? When? What happened?

What are your fears about the OCD?

Have you sacrificed anything for "Peace at any price?" What? Has that goal made your life unmanageable? How?

Keeping a journal is a very good way to get in touch with your feelings. Scheduling a private, uninterrupted, daily time to write in your journal, notebook or diary is a way to take some time for yourself. A journal can be used in so many ways: as a record of daily events which are so easily forgotten, as a source to note how you feel about and handle situations and a place to write down your goals and hopes so that you can remember them. Writing can also be a way to "dump" feelings that feel too destructive to say, or that you are afraid to share. Seeing them in print gives you a certain distance from them and helps you decide what to do. Uncensored, free writing with no concern for grammar or style is an excellent way to tap your unconscious and find out what's really going on. Try it; you may be surprised!

Facing OCD brings family issues up and makes roles clear. It's a good time to resolve old conflicts and change roles that you don't like. Your recovery is not just about detaching and not enabling; it's about enjoying your life and relationships and becoming the person you were meant to be before the illness struck.

One change that you can make immediately is toward direct communication. Triangles are common in troubled families; one person speaks to another about a third. Triangles are very stressful. Break them by speaking directly to the person involved without dragging someone else in, especially a child. Refuse to engage in negative discussions about someone who is not present.

Use "I" messages: "I think... I feel... I see... I don't know..." "I" messages are assertive, not aggressive. This technique goes far toward healing the damaging atmosphere of blame that may have existed for a long time. Notice how you feel when someone starts a sentence with "You..." Most people in a conflict-resolving session feel defensive when "You.." statements are made especially if "You always..." or "You never..." accusations are made. Think about it: "Always" and "never" are unfair absolutes that can be disputed with *one* example to the contrary. This leads to arguments and a betrayal of personal responsibility: No one can *make* someone else feel a certain way. Feelings are personal responses and cannot be controlled by other people.

In family discussions, it may be safer to have a neutral moderator or counselor present to make sure everyone is heard and that the focus is on topics, not character-bashing. It is also important to listen carefully and understand that what you heard is what the person meant. A counselor or therapist can ask questions to see if people are really hearing each other instead of just waiting their turns to respond. Also, focusing on the present moment and planning for the future are more helpful than rehashing the past. What's done is done, and in order to heal, the family needs to move toward forgiveness of the OCD, and the PWOCD and each other.

Forgiveness is very healing. This may not be possible for you right now, but eventually, as an experiment, try forgiving the OCD. OCD has no meaning besides medical facts. It is not a punishment. No one caused it. It doesn't have to be melodramatic, or karmic, or an excuse to give up. It is not a test of "character." It just *is*. If you do not feel very forgiving right now, refrain from judging yourself for that. There is no "right" way to heal.

Healing takes time. Change in families is gradual. Not every-thing can be resolved. It's okay to "let a mess be a mess" until people work things out, if and when they are ready.

Boundaries are also important for family recovery. Some boundary habits are easy to learn, like knocking on closed doors and not interrupting people when they are speaking. Other boundaries are more subtle: Living with OCD creates an emotion-ally charged situation in which your needs are so intertwined with the needs of the PWOCD that yours get lost. In a boundaryless state, your happiness is contingent on his moods and the state of his symptoms. Family members often feel "smaller" than the OCD and their world typically shrinks around "the Problem."

One solution: *Get out for a while and do things you like to do.* Take a walk, see a movie, meet a friend for lunch, go shopping or dancing, volunteer or take a part-time job or a class; do something you've always wanted to do! Write a letter, start a garden or create a quiet corner in your house just for you where you can retreat and do solitary activities like sewing, reading or listening to music. Decorate your special room or corner with things you find beauti-ful. Make it comfortable and inspirational for you. If you are pressed for space, a long hot bath can do wonders to recharge and relax you.

"First Things First" as they say in AA: How long has it been since you have gone to the doctor or dentist for a checkup? When was the last time you bought a new pair of shoes or had your hair done? Even if you don't feel happy and secure, cultivating your appearance, eating well and getting some exercise will make you feel better. Even buying yourself flowers sends a message inside that you are beginning to take care of *you.* A good method is to treat yourself at least as well as the person you care about.

If you are willing to change being driven by the behavior of the PWOCD, you are able to escape the manipulative and manipu-lated, victimized mentality of the average troubled family. You can start to discover your own needs. In order to know what you need, you have to find out how you feel. Be patient, it may take a while for your feelings to "thaw" after being hidden from the embattled state of trying to control OCD.

Remember, you are not abandoning the PWOCD by focusing on yourself, even if at times they vent self pity and anger in your direction. Be direct and tell them that you need some time alone and that you'll be back. Detachment is not a wall, it is a bridge back to your own feelings and *appropriate* responsibility for yourself and others. *A relapse for the PWOCD can be obvious, but what constitutes a relapse for you? How about a reappearance of the idea that you are responsible for the PWOCD's behavior and results?*

In order to communicate honestly with the PWOCD you need to know how you are feeling. At first, most of us felt only numb a good deal of the time. Get in the habit of asking yourself what you are feeling. Give it a name. Always try to be very specific when you describe a feeling, whether it is hurt, hopefulness, boredom, annoyance, calm or another of the thousands of emotions and admixtures we can feel.

The next part is just to feel it. Accept it for what it is. Observe it. What parts of your body do you feel it in? How is it changing? Is it passing?

The most powerful tool is to start saying how you feel.

If you know what you feel, then you can find out what you need. The HALT concept from Alcoholics Anonymous can be a guide: "Never get too *H*ungry, *A*ngry, *L*onely or *T*ired." If you are hungry, eat; if you are tired, get some sleep soon and if you are lonely it's time to talk to someone. The telephone is your lifeline to sanity and as uncomfortable as it feels at first, make an effort to call people from your support group or whom you find to be understanding and willing to listen. A support group meeting is also a good way to remedy loneliness. It is a fact of life, though, that a certain amount of loneliness seems to be part of "the human condition," so don't give yourself a hard time for being lonely once in a while. This is where a spiritual connection can really help.

What about anger? Along with guilt, anger is a common companion for family members of PWOCD. Does HALT mean you are not allowed to feel angry? Of course not; you are allowed to feel any way that you feel. Feelings are not good or bad, they just are. Anger can be frightening because it is usually a response to a fear of some kind. If you look behind anger, you will often find a fear. Are you angry at the PWOCD because you spend so much time taking them to doctors? Or the opposite: Maybe they won't go for help. That means you are probably afraid that you are missing out on your life. Behind every fear is a need. If you are afraid you are spending too much time with PWOCD, you need more time for yourself.

How can you get what you need? It may seem impossible with the current obstacles you perceive. What are those obstacles? Try making a list of them. How can you get around them? Is it that you feel there is "no one else" to take care of the PWOCD? Living in an isolated, controlled situation as we did with OCD makes it difficult for most of us to ask for help. If you can allow the idea that you can ask for help, you can begin to make positive changes and feel more confident. "Time off" can make you more effective when you return, and more pleasant to be around, too!

Even if family members and friends are unavailable or uncooperative, even if you haven't made it to support meetings to make contacts who can help you, and even if you think you can't afford therapy for yourself to help you make changes, there are other resources available. Community organizations such as the United Way offer free services to homebound or dependent PWOCD such as transportation services, Adult day and foster care, home health care, counseling, chore services, Meals on Wheels, housekeeping, companion and visitor services. Call the OC Foundation, social service agencies, public health services, mental health agencies, community organizations, the National Self-Help Clearinghouse, churches and synagogues, hospitals and YMCA's and YWCA's to see what is available in your area. There is no problem so great that it cannot be addressed and there is no reason to be alone with a problem.

"Something happened to me that hurt and changed me. What happened was not my fault, but I can do something about the changes in me, and I can stop hurting."

> — Al-Anon Member, *Al-Anon Faces Alcoholism, 2nd Edition* [11.]

You have probably noticed that this book contains much Twelve-Step program orientation towards recovering and problem solving for friends and families of PWOCD. If you have not thrown it across the room by now, you likely have some acceptance of "anonymous" therapeutic concepts or are at least willing to hear them out. If you have attended Al-Anon, CODA or OC-Anon meetings and do not wish to return, let's explore some objections you may have and offer you some options.

1. "I want to handle this by myself. It's no one's business." Explore the disadvantages of carrying the burden by yourself.

2. "My life is not as terrible as the stories I heard. I don't belong in the group." Pain is relative and cannot be compared or measured. Neglect and non-events can be more subtle to express, but just as painful as blatant abuse and disruption.

3. "The God stuff turns me off. I don't believe in religion." Explore past experiences in which faith in someone or something besides yourself was helpful. "Take what you need and leave the rest" is a useful slogan from AA. No one is insisting that you believe anything.

4. "It's so ritualistic. I hate all that clapping and it's embarrassing to say my name and hear everyone say 'Hello _____'" Explore issues of acknowledgment. Why has it not been safe to be noticed before? You can also ask people not to clap or say "Hello _____" until you are ready.

The best way to use a support group is to speak openly: Tell the truth about your life right now. All of your feelings are important and deserve discussion. Give the people in the meetings a chance to get to know you so they can help. Admit the problem and be willing to support others by listening. Silence your inner critic for the duration of the meeting and really try to hear the feelings people are expressing, even if you disagree with or don't understand what they are saying. Accept help: Often the one person in the room whom you are sure you won't like says the things you most need to hear. Ask for help in reaching your goals by asking the group if the members can tell you how they handled the specific problem you are experiencing.

No matter what you may think of a meeting or certain people in it, in a support group, you are no longer alone. You are just as important as everyone else in the group and you deserve support. You are worth listening to. Going to meetings connects you with others, especially if you work on dropping those defenses that keep you so "safe" and isolated!

If you do not "get called on" or there is not enough time to share in depth, ask a sponsor or counselor to listen or to help you in a more detailed and personal way. A sponsor can help you with your "hands-off" program for the PWOCD, by pointing out relapses and redirecting your focus to yourself. A sponsor is a nonprofessional guide and the relationship is informal, subject to termination by either party.

All of this recovery work is well and good, but there are times when you and the PWOCD will both want to take a break from intense emotions. You do not have to dwell constantly on recovering from OCD. Put it away at times to expand your interests, have fun and talk about other things. Include the person with OCD in family activities that everyone enjoys. "Meeting life on life's terms" means experiencing each moment, letting it fill you and letting it go.

Sometimes we do not know what is going on. We don't have to have all the answers. We don't know why we can't cure OCD and sometimes it's better to stop talking and just be together. OCD does not end life, it redirects life. The experience can be a positive one in that it makes us more sensitive to our real priorities and the importance of the people we love. In the end, the best way you can help people with OCD is to accept them. Be who *you* are and *you* will find your answers in your own heart.

The Twelve Steps for Families

Our recovery program adapts the Twelve Steps of Alcoholics Anonymous for families and friends affected by a loved one's OCD. The reason we use the Twelve Steps is because we have found that they work. The Twelve Steps are our keys to a new life. Even when we doubted the program would work, or thought *we* certainly didn't need a program, we discovered it was worth a try. After all, our own ideas for coping with the illness of OCD in our loved ones had not brought us relief. By following the program suggestions, we got results. This is a program of *action*, however. It works when we do the work and take the necessary actions, with the help of recovering friends and a Greater Power.

It's easy and natural to focus blame on the disease of OCD. At one time or another we have all hated the disease as we watched it steal people, love and dreams. Unfortunately, it is also common to blame the person with OCD. Few of us had considered what we might have done to make the situation worse. We have found that there are many personality traits and attributes in families and relationships that actually fuel the OCD. By working a Twelve-Step program of recovery, we can examine *our* roles in the unhappy situation.

This program is not about blaming ourselves and feeling guilty. It is about taking an honest look at the whole picture. Even making a beginning on this process creates a new, liberating way of thinking: *We are not victims.* Conflicts do not happen because of one person. We are involved and our actions have an effect.

A Twelve-Step inventory of our character traits, paradoxically, helps us to *take* control by letting go of control. Taking stock of how *we* have contributed to any situation and beginning to change the things we need to in *ourselves* restores our true power to us.

43

Here are the steps that outline our program:

Step 1. We admitted that we were powerless over anyone's obsessions and compulsions — that our lives had become unmanageable.

Step 2. Came to believe that a Power greater than ourselves could restore us to sanity.

Step 3. Made a decision to turn our will and our lives over to the care of God *as we understood Him.*

Step 4. Made a searching and fearless moral inventory of ourselves.

Step 5. Admitted to God, to ourselves, and to another human being the exact nature of our wrongs.

Step 6. Were entirely ready to have God remove all these defects of character.

Step 7. Humbly asked Him to remove our shortcomings.

Step 8. Made a list of all persons we had harmed and became willing to make amends to them all.

Step 9. Made direct amends to such people wherever possible, except when to do so would injure them or others.

Step 10. Continued to take personal inventory and when we were wrong promptly admitted it.

Step 11. Sought through prayer and meditation to improve our conscious contact with God *as we understood Him,* praying only for knowledge of His will for us and the power to carry that out.

Step 12. Having had a spiritual awakening as a result of these steps, we tried to carry this message to others, and to practice these principles in all our affairs.

44

The Twelve Steps of AA

1. We admitted we were powerless over alcohol — that our lives had become unmanageable.

2. Came to believe that a Power greater than ourselves could restore us to sanity.

3. Made a decision to turn our will and our lives over to the care of God, *as we understood Him.*

4. Made a searching and fearless moral inventory of ourselves.

5. Admitted to God, to ourselves, and to another human being the exact nature of our wrongs.

6. Were entirely ready to have God remove all these defects of character.

7. Humbly asked Him to remove our shortcomings.

8. Made a list of all persons we had harmed and became willing to make amends to them all.

9. Made direct amends to such people wherever possible, except when to do so would injure them or others.

10. Continued to take personal inventory and when we were wrong promptly admitted it.

11. Sought through prayer and meditation to improve our conscious contact with God *as we understood Him,* praying only for knowledge of His will for us and the power to carry that out.

12. Having had a spiritual awakening as a result of these steps, we tried to carry this message to alcoholics and to practice these principles in all our affairs.

The Twelve Steps are reprinted and adapted with permission of Alcoholics Anonymous World Services, Inc. Permission to reprint and adapt this material does not mean that AA has reviewed or approved the contents of this publication, nor that AA agrees with the views expressed herein. AA is a program of recovery from alcoholism *only* - use of the Twelve Steps in connection with programs and activities which are patterned after AA, but which address other problems, does not imply otherwise.

Step 1. *We admitted we were powerless over anyone's obsessions and compulsions — that our lives had become unmanageable.* There is a reason why this is the first step. Without a true acceptance of Step One, none of the other steps are very useful. The meaning of Step One is understood on a gut level as the feelings that bring people into a program of recovery; defeat, powerlessness and the realization that no amount of control, denial, rescuing, anger, bargains or sadness changed the situation. In fact, it was getting worse. It is very hard for most of us to admit that it is impossible to control OCD.

OCD is incredibly powerful. Any direct attempt to defeat it is a losing battle. Recovery is not a matter of willpower, advanced techniques or interpersonal schemes to control the PWOCD. Unaided effort has failed us all. No amount of human will power can break the obsessions and compulsions of the PWOCD. Acceptance that we cannot negotiate with the symptoms is our admission of powerlessness.

It doesn't matter how the OCD gained control. It did. Its power made our lives unmanageable. Unmanageability does not necessarily mean we lost good jobs, nice homes or families, though some did. Not being able to enjoy life was unmanageable enough. This private pain was enough to get us to take the first step.

Admitting powerlessness and noting the areas of our lives that have become unmanageable means that we surrender. Surrendering, in this case, is not the same as giving up. Miraculously, by surrendering to the truth of the disease, we can begin to take back some of our real power and authority as far as *we* are concerned. Because we, as well as the PWOCD, are also powerless over the

OCD. Negotiating with the symptoms, enabling the sufferer and making bargains and deals are all a waste of time and, in fact, contributed to the unmanageability in our lives.

The best way to deal with a loved one's OCD is to *ignore the obsessions* and not allow yourself to feed into the disease. This attitude of detachment will help you whether the PWOCD is in recovery or not. We are not abandoning the PWOCD — we are simply not giving the disease any more power by participating in answering obsessive questions or engaging in rituals. We are not giving up on them; we are giving up trying to control them.

Surrendering control and working Step One involve a change in focus, a willingness to look within and see how we have been affected by the OCD. Only by getting a clear picture of its impact can we receive the ability to change our lives.

Step 2. *Came to believe that a Power greater than ourselves could restore us to sanity.* Here is the hope. Once we tried Step One, most of us felt we were left hanging. "Okay, I surrender. And now what?"

Step Two is the answer. It means we were doing things which felt insane because they didn't work, or made us feel worse, yet we kept doing them. Coming to believe occurred when we met and listened to people who had been in as much pain as we were and who have found a measure of peace and happiness. These people provide hope. A Power greater than ourselves provides help.

At first, many of us found this step inconceivable. It asks us to believe something that has no proof of existing. We were told to believe it until we felt it, or "act as if," which seemed backward. Some of us had believed in a Higher Power at one time, but felt disappointed or even abused by religion. The Twelve Steps embody a spiritual program, not a religion. Each person conceives his spiritual source in a personal way.

For some reason, the *belief* in a Greater Power's ability to restore us to sanity is enough to begin the process. When we stopped debating the sense of this step, its benefits gradually came to us.

For those of us for whom belief in a transcendent or disembodied power is not possible, we found making the support group our Higher Power has worked just as well. Clearly, the group has had better results recovering from the battleground of OCD than we did on our own. We can trust in the *principles* of the program, working through group consciousness, to safely guide us. Coming to believe is a process we can experience to the best of our ability with acceptance for where we are right now.

Step 3. *Made a decision to turn our will and our lives over to the care of God as we understood Him.* This step is not as complicated as it sounds. Didn't we already turn our will over to the OCD and the chaos and suffering it caused? That plan didn't work too well. And we have already begun the essence of Step Three by seeking help. Merely by reading this book or attending a meeting, you are putting aside self will long enough to receive guidance from sources outside yourself.

This step alarmed many of us: "What? Turn my *life* over to something I can't even see? No way!"

It invoked an extreme vision of passivity that seemed absurd, impractical and even dangerous. This step is not as extreme as all that. It is not about being a martyr; it is an invitation to open ourselves up to a larger plan, a personal plan "beyond our wildest dreams."

One of the paradoxes of Step Three is that the more we depend on a Higher Power to handle those things which baffle us, the happier and more independent we become. The past has shown us that our rigid rules for living with the PWOCD have brought only remorse, guilt and loneliness. Step Three is the solution to the misuse of willpower. When we step back and "get out of our own way," better answers tend to come from sources we had been too busy to hear.

Working Step Three does not mean we do not make decisions, or that we wait for a "sign" before doing anything. We ask for help, for often a Higher Power speaks through others. We take actions and let go of the results. It is a lot easier to enjoy life when we do not try to control the outcome of everything. That is what is meant by "living life on life's terms."

Step Three is enhanced with the Serenity Prayer: "God grant me the serenity to accept the things I cannot change, courage to change the things I can and the wisdom to know the difference." When we are in need of willingness to work Step Three we can affirm that God's will, not ours, be done.

Step 4. *Made a searching and fearless moral inventory of ourselves.* The purpose of an inventory is to find out what our personal supplies are. It answers the questions: What are we working with? What is useful? What isn't? The code for accessing our emotional inventory is a list of resentments. This list, especially if done in the chart form recommended in this step, helps us to see who we resent and why and how the resentments affect us. Usually, a pattern emerges and it becomes easier to see what our role might be and what part we play in these conflicts.

A moral inventory is fearless, but not ruthless. Objectivity is important. There are other aspects to consider such as the damage done to ourselves by lack of self-love, accumulated guilt, hurts and angers. The issues of when we have made ourselves too important and when not important enough also arise. Ultimately, the Fourth Step inventory helps us set new standards for ourselves, fair, human, appropriate standards. It is also our guide to discarding rigid rules and self-judgments.

Step Four is a way to put down the "emotional baggage" of our liabilities. Many of us thought we were defect-free, except in response to the PWOCD, and if only *they* were to change, we would be fine. Others of us thought there was nothing wrong with our behavior or, conversely, that *everything* we did was wrong and we were somehow to blame for the OCD problems.

Starting with a written list of resentments is the easiest way for many of us to begin because resentments are usually "up front" and easy to remember.

A suggested approach:

I'm resentful at: (People, Institutions, or principles)	The Cause: (Why we were angry)	Affects my:
Mr. Doe	Unreasonable boss Doesn't appreciate my abilities	May lose job Self-esteem (fear)
Myself	Nagging behavior	Self-esteem (fear)
My spouse	Obsessive- compulsive	Pride Sex relations

This list immediately reveals the effect of resentments on our lives.

Another approach is to use the "Seven Deadly Sins" of pride, greed, lust, anger, gluttony, envy and sloth as categories to gauge our behavior. Pride and "justified anger" at a cruel world are stumbling blocks to personal honesty. Feeling deprived can justify selfishness and self pity and we may not want to examine how we take out our frustrations on others. These behaviors hinder spiritual growth and get in the way of recovery.

It is also helpful to write a list of our fears. Fears are often behind much of the behavior we don't like and which cause trouble with others. Fear of losing what we have or not getting what we want leads to self-centeredness. Faith is the answer here; trust that a Higher Power is guiding us, meeting our needs, removing harmful dependencies and providing things we didn't even know we wanted.

Sex conduct is another inventory that can be dealt with on the Fourth Step list. Look for anger, resentments and jealousy and remember those times we used sex to punish others, whether by withholding it, having affairs or flirting outside the relationship.

We often find that asking ourselves, "Did I act selfishly?" can clarify the issue.

Relationships with family and close friends can be inventoried in terms of how we used dependency or domination. Both of these traits are self-centered and lead to unequal, disharmonious relationships. A clear picture of how we have related to people can help us have relationships that are partnerships, rather than power struggles.

In terms of the OCD-related inventory, specifically, there are certain family personality traits which have been found to fuel the OCD. If any of these traits sound familiar, it can be included on the Fourth Step list. One of the most common environments that fosters OCD is that of the *controlling or smothering family*. Those of us with these attitudes did not permit freedom for our loved ones. We demanded perfection from them and were insensitive to their needs. We didn't give them much quality time, yet we were overprotective, causing them to fear separation from us. The guilt and anger that resulted helped fuel their OCD rituals.

The opposite situation, that of the *absentee family*, is just as common for people with OCD. Those of us who weren't there for our children did not satisfy their need to be nurtured. They tried to be perfect, hoping they would be reunited with us if they were "good enough." An actual separation from us at a formative time in their lives made them afraid of being abandoned by other people later in life. Child abandonment issues are one of the triggers for OCD. Repressed feelings of anger and dependency toward parents can surface in the mid-twenties or thirties in the form of OCD. As with all possible OCD triggers, it is important to discuss your family history with your therapist.

In the family with *high expectations* there is a lot of guilt. Children have no way of knowing these expectations are unrealistic. They grow up with a doomed feeling; they are always mad at themselves for "not getting enough done." The defect of having *perfectionist expectations* breeds compulsive personalities. As perfectionist parents, we expected our children to get straight A's,

51

have good table manners, never embarrass us or lose our tempers and never fight with their siblings. Our children likely grew up with low self esteem and perpetual self-criticism, even when they are successful. Other traits are over-commitment, nit-picking, competitiveness, an inability to relax and, of course, perfectionism.

Other *perfectionist* defects are telling children to be quiet and not to complain; they "should" feel fortunate. Some of us did not allow children to express fears or disappointments. With love conditional on performance and no relief valve for insecurity, many children are led to OCD.

Additional traits common to families of people with OCD are: talking too much and not listening to the child, expecting performances beyond the level of the child's age and coordination, introversion, fault-finding and being critical of others, snobbery, fostering competition, lack of spiritual beliefs, ignoring limits set for children by our spouse or not following through on consequences determined by our spouse, miserliness with money, affection and time, rigid rules and sexual shaming or secrecy.

The solution is to love the child unconditionally. Give a lot of physical hugs. Listen to their feelings and encourage them to express feelings without fear of punishment, even if they are angry at *us.* If they feel insecure, tell them it's okay; they can talk about it. Spend a lot of time really listening to them.

If their report card is less than perfect, and they made an adequate effort, praise them for what they achieved. Don't criticize them for the few things they didn't do as well. If we put the standards within reach, our children will reach them. If they know it's possible to satisfy us, they won't have to be compulsive to do it.

Hidden anger behind all of the issues we have discussed is the key to the recovery process for the family. This step is worth some time and attention. Interestingly, it is the step most of us procrastinated about doing. Many of us delayed it with justifications and rationalizations, but that only delays the profound insight and deep relief the Fourth Step brings. It is worth doing in order to come up with a concise list of defects and assets. Remember to list your good qualities. A clear idea of how you operate will be your guide to change, self-acceptance and a life-long process of reliable self-evaluation with the Tenth Step.

Step 5. *Admitted to God, to ourselves, and to another human being the exact nature of our wrongs.* This is the house-cleaning step. Here we got to dump all the garbage we've been carrying by telling our "worst secrets" to a trusted person. It was time to become free of the secrecy surrounding our relationship with the PWOCD. By doing the Fifth Step, we gave it all away to someone who has been there and didn't judge us for what we had to say. Experiencing their objective view and forgiveness was very healing. We began to break out of the isolation, shame and guilt of the secrets.

The relief we felt from the Fifth Step comes from being honest, experiencing humility and trusting God, as well as another person. We got a realistic idea of our true assets and shortcomings, as opposed to exaggerated ideas fed by the drama of our troubled relationships and magnified roles.

The Fifth Step brings great relief. We are no longer alone. We are no longer carrying such a heavy load of guilt and shame. We are able to shift our focus to larger concerns and we can let people into our world.

Step 6. *Were entirely ready to have God remove all these defects of character.* Step Six is about dealing with the solutions which became our problems. Defects of character are really just behaviors which worked or had some benefit in a troubled situation. That is why some people in the program say that "defects are just assets turned inside out." In recovery, many of these solutions become burdensome or inappropriate, which speeds our willingness to change.

Working on the Sixth Step is a daily program of willingness to change. It looks easier than it is. Some defects have payoffs we are not ready to let go of and others are just comfortable. We may not yet trust that we know how to live without them. Being ready to let go of defects does not mean they are automatically and permanently removed. A process of patient improvement will lead to a new freedom from old defects of character.

In order for us to become entirely ready to confront our shortcomings, we can re-acquaint ourselves with our Fourth Step inventory. *Perfectionism* is a trait we see a lot of. It causes painful feelings of impossibility, anxiety, stress and unhappiness until we attain a measure of faith in a Higher Power, acceptance of ourselves and a relaxing of control.

Self-righteous anger and *blaming* may give short-term relief, but in the long run, they make us feel stuck. Blaming OCD, the PWOCD or ourselves for everything is just a symptom of pride and the reverse-pride of grandiose self-pity. Acceptance of ourselves where we are right now is the key to recovery.

Self pity is a ride to nowhere. Whining, "It's not fair!" and "Why does my family member have OCD?" makes us feel like the weight of the world is upon us, when really, what we need is to get perspective to be our right size. Self pity is just a manifestation of *grandiosity*. It's as if we are so important that we merit extra universal attention, positive or negative. The truth is that *everyone* has problems, and this one happens to be ours. While we are not responsible for our troubled thinking that developed in response to the OCD, we *are* responsible to change and grow. One solution that works well when self pity appears is to be of service and help others.

Inflexibility keeps us in destructive relationships. We do not have to stay in situations that feed our fear of intimacy, workaholism or tendency to deny our feelings. It takes courage to look at each relationship and decide whether to end it or try to repair it. Especially in early recovery, we need to put ourselves first. Some people dislike it when you say "No" because it means they can no longer use you. For a long time, many of us did not know *who we were* unless we were needed. In a strange way, this also made us feel that we controlled the other person, though neither of us got what we needed. Be prepared for some resistance from others and perhaps, residual guilt within yourself when you first start saying "No." You can use the program to support your boundaries.

Excessive and destructive *control* of other people and the environment is self-defeating behavior that we developed in response to feeling controlled by others and by OCD. In order to ease out of this situation, we need to set boundaries and stick to them. Most of us had a history of making threats that were ignored. We needed to declare our emotional independence. This takes courage and patience, but it leads to freedom and personal integrity. There is no excuse to accept abuse or to abuse anyone. Action and change come with this program of recovery. The process of acknowledging defects is one of daily observation. Getting ready to let go of defects prepares us for Step Seven.

Step 7. *Humbly asked Him to remove our shortcomings.* "Humbly" is the operative word here. Humility means changing in pace with a larger plan. Some changes happen quickly, but others are long in coming. It often happens that our priorities are different than we once thought. As we change, so does our perception of the Seventh Step and our faith in a Higher Power's timetable for removing our shortcomings and providing new guidance.

The feeling of Step Seven is related to Step One where we admitted defeat and turned to a Higher Power. In time, self-centered fear and superficial values are healed with humility. When we let God's will in and put aside our constant demands, we make room for spiritual values. Our former misery is transformed and strength comes out of weakness. The removal of our shortcomings ultimately benefits everyone as we grow to be of better service to ourselves and others.

Step 8. *Made a list of all persons we had harmed, and became willing to make amends to them all.* Becoming willing requires a continuation of humility as we experienced it in the other steps. Step Eight is not a guilt-inducing step. It actually removes guilt's hold on our lives. Remember to put yourself on your amends list!

55

The charts and lists we made while doing the Fourth Step helped us find the people we had harmed. Our natural tendency is to go on the defensive when thinking about a personal conflict. It seems so important for us to prove we were "right." The fact is that strained relationships bring out the worst in both parties, even if we feel we were only *reacting* to someone else's negative behavior. We are responsible for what we said and did, including those things we should have said or done, but did not. In order to recover, we must own up to our part and become willing to make amends.

Some forms of harm are subtle. Emotional and spiritual harm we have inflicted was a burden to us in ways we had not previously explored. Many of us can recall being inflexible, callous, critical, impatient, humorless, martyred, or lashing out in frustration at the OCD. Others may even have tolerated this because that's just "how we are." We need to first forgive ourselves. Then, making amends will free us from those resentments.

Some amends cannot be made. The people we have harmed are gone, unavailable or completely unreceptive. In these cases, a private amend can be prepared for prayer or writing, not to be sent. Some amends have to be deferred for other reasons, which can be weighed in introspection and by sharing in meetings or with a trusted person. It is important not to bring perfectionism or drama into this process of list-making. This list does not have to begin at your birth or have hundreds of names on it. There may be only a few names on your list. When we avoid extreme thinking or exaggeration the task at hand becomes simple.

Step 9. *Made direct amends to such people wherever possible, except when to do so would injure them or others.* The Ninth Step is very simple and very effective. Just make sure you do not injure *yourself,* either. No matter how we may feel about the harm we have done, making amends does not mean crawling before another person, or exposing ourselves to abuse or a re-creation of the situation. We are entitled to live in human dignity, with compassion for ourselves and others. Discuss uncertain amends with a suppor-

56

tive person who knows you well enough to help you make sure they are warranted.

In this step, we washed away the past and "came clean" of our old resentments. Repairing the damage of the past frees us into emotional sobriety. While some people were receptive to our amends, others didn't know there was a problem; it seems the resentment was one-sided. Suddenly, the stored grudge was defused, which helped us forgive ourselves because it was not such a "big deal" as we thought.

In making restitution for cheating, lies or theft of some sort, it is important to be honest and fair, but not to make the situation worse. If the people or person involved knows of the deception, we can make a direct amend and financial restitution or arrangement, if necessary. There is no point in going into detail or revealing names involved in extra-marital affairs if our partners did not know about them. Likewise, if padding an expense account was not suspected, it is important not to create bad feelings or further injury. Guidance from a Higher Power and advice from those experienced in the program can help you decide how to handle these situations.

Step 10. *Continued to take personal inventory and when we were wrong promptly admitted it.* The Tenth Step is an ongoing process of evaluating our days. We look for reasons to congratulate ourselves or to change certain behaviors. It's important to stay with today and not to let residual guilt affect this practice. Get rid of any new guilt by taking care of the situation immediately.

When we survey our daily attitudes, whether in writing or reflection, we create a daily balance sheet of assets as well as shortcomings such as inflexibility or self-centeredness. Feelings of anger, resentment or fear are clues to situations that may warrant a Tenth Step inventory. This can also be done informally as part of a daily journal or on the telephone with a sponsor. If this process seems time-consuming, it may help to know that we have found it actually *saves* time by nipping problems in the bud and increasing our kindness and tolerance towards others.

Any uncomfortable feelings we have during the day can be addressed by a spot-check mental inventory. We ask ourselves what our part is in the conflict and if any of our known defects could be involved. Difficult times call for self-restraint and a willingness to admit our part. It is important to avoid arguments, criticism and sulking.

Resentments are often caused by having too-high expectations of other people. It is important to ask ourselves if those expectations are realistic and fair or if we are asking too much of the person. Remember that we each have our own "row to hoe." Others are also living in this difficult world of ours and doing the best they can.

In drawing up a daily balance sheet, we also list assets or esteemable actions so we can gauge our progress. We watch out for motives behind our actions to keep an eye on selfishness. Attempts to change or control people to get them to "see it our way" are relapse behaviors for us. Self-righteousness has no place when we honestly know we are being self-centered. Likewise, justification only confuses the situation and makes it harder to resolve.

An honest attempt to work the Tenth Step reduces our problems and aligns a higher plan for us.

Step 11. *Sought through prayer and meditation to improve our conscious contact with God as we understood Him, praying only for knowledge of His will for us and the power to carry that out.* This is a life-long step. Many of us needed to learn the difference between meditation and rumination. Rumination does not bring about positive changes in our consciousness and level of serenity. In fact, it traps us in circular thinking. Meditation is a process of relaxing *away* from thoughts and emptying one's mind. One way to understand meditation is to compare it to prayer: "Prayer is talking; meditation is listening," as they say in the program. Meditating is about trusting our Higher Power and the answers that come in silence. In the process, we learn to trust ourselves.

Many agnostics and atheists who find prayer an alien concept are able to find relief in the related practices of self-examination and meditation. Even if prayer seems impractical, experimenting with prayer and meditation "just for today" often leads to valuable, unexpected results, without committing to a life-time practice.

Asking for specific things or results in prayer defeats the purpose of aligning our will with a Higher Power's will for us. As we do not know what is in store for us, it is better to request, "Thy will, not mine, be done." Prayers are often answered in unexpected ways, through mediums that we were unaware of. It is wiser to watch for these answers, rather than to "make bargains" with God. By including our Higher Power in our daily dialogue we no longer feel alone in a hostile world. We have support and guidance in ways we could not previously imagine.

Step 12. *Having had a spiritual awakening as a result of these steps, we tried to carry this message to others, and to practice these principles in all our affairs.* A spiritual awakening leads to true love of oneself and others. A spiritual awakening is not a visionary of "white light" experience for most of us. It is a gradual shifting of inner priorities and values. The process is personally meaningful and cannot always be explained. We have a source of serenity that we can tap at any time. We are no longer isolated when the Twelfth Step puts us in contact with others who uniquely understand

We carry the message to those in the lonely prison of secrecy and defeat which limits them in their relationship to a PWOCD. Carrying the message does not mean convincing or preaching. If a message a suffering person needs to hear comes through us, it is because we were in the right place at the right time. If not, perhaps the next person they meet will be able to help. Working the Twelfth Step also means living well and taking care of ourselves. When we do this, it shows and others are attracted.

A spiritual program works in all areas of life. Daily practice of this program carries itself into all other aspects of life in an attitude of increased acceptance and helpfulness and decreased self-seeking. We have seen that trying to manipulate people and situations did not work, but when we change from the inside and think about how we can help others, our world becomes a better place.

The program also changes isolated living and previously dependent relationships into true partnerships with others. Trust and openness to new situations and ideas mean we can share our burdens and have more time to enjoy our lives.

We will close this introduction to the Twelve Steps by saying the program is not a theory; we have to live it if we want recovery in our lives. Progress is what we strive for and, in time, our problems with people with OCD will be relieved if we give this way of life a chance to work for us.

A Personal Viewpoint

Much has been written about detaching with love. This is especially important if your *parents* have OCD. A child raised in this family environment can feel the brutal effects of a parent with the illness. Much of the time, the child feels *trapped* in the family illness and also a victim of a controlling environment. There is little room for independence since the parent can also incorporate the child into the illness. Little freedom of expression is allowed and often the child will be asked to participate in the *rituals themselves.*

To recover, the child must accept that their parent has an illness and that the child didn't cause it. As adults they can learn to apply the steps in their lives to grow away from the illness.

If your spouse has OCD, much of this book will prove helpful, especially the steps and the practice of detaching with love. If your child has OCD, perhaps my story will help also.

Father and Daughter —
Our Recoveries from OCD

I know of fewer things more painful than suffering from OCD. I also know that when something happens to one's child the pain is also intense. But it is when you have OCD and your child suddenly gets OCD that life gets real.

My earliest childhood memories consisted of OCD. I remember my room having specific places for specific toys which I would not permit others to disturb. Counting and checking rituals became staples in my daily activities and others soon began to take a curious notice. My kindergarten teacher dubbed me with the nickname of "Repeat" because I often found it necessary to "repeat" what she had just said.

My OCD continued into adolescence and adulthood, having a major effect on my happiness, but minimal effect on my external success. I graduated from professional school and managed to do well in the working world. My OCD at this time consisted of the earlier mentioned behaviors as well as a newly acquired ritual: daily skin picking of blemishes.

I am fortunate to be in recovery today. My recovery from OCD continues to be strong and I attribute this success primarily to the Twelve-Step program of Obsessive Compulsive Anonymous, as well as to the caring professionals who have helped me. I believe that this combination was my way out of the OCD maze.

Just as things had fallen into place for me, I had an experience I can only describe as terrifying. My four-year-old daughter had an acute OCD episode that lasted three months. This beautiful, brilliant little girl who loved life had become consumed with the fear that she "maybe was hurting other people." Her questioning and repeating was endless: "Mommy, did I poke you in the eyes with my fork when I was eating dinner?" "Daddy, I'm afraid to go to nursery school because I might step on someone's toes or bump into them and hurt them."

We were fortunate — we knew that this was OCD even though I never had any of her fears of hurting others. We also knew that waiting for it to go away by itself wasn't going to help. Today my daughter is symptom free and I can attribute her remarkable recovery to several factors:

1. *Good doctors* — Specifically, behavior therapy exposure/response prevention in action. We were told *not* to answer her obsessive questions and to send her off to school kicking and screaming if necessary. Her obsessive questions were essentially ignored and she was *not* permitted to isolate from life. We found this, at times, difficult but we were told it would help over time. When she asked if she hurt her baby brother when she kissed him we told her we don't answer "silly questions."

2. *Our support* — At no time was our daughter made to feel guilty for her behavior. She was told that her Daddy also had these "silly thoughts" and that she would get better like her father did.

3. *Change in lifestyle* — We found that although we didn't cause our daughter's OCD there were things we could change to help her. Being perfectionistic, we tended to formulate a code of behavior which was contraindicated for someone prone to OCD. Our relatively rigid rules about neatness, personal safety and cleanliness were thrown out the window. We now allowed our child to make mistakes she was entitled to make. No longer did we follow her every move — within reason, she was allowed to make a mess, play outside like the other kids and get dirty through and through. Our original policy of being "safe rather than sorry" was replaced with "change rather than OCD."

We also found that *our* relationship needed some work, which it did receive. We believe it was *no coincidence* that our daughter's OCD episode was directly preceded by a severe and threatening argument between her parents.

4. *Fate* — Just maybe we had to go through this pain so that we could tell others what we did and how it is working for us today. From our experience others can now benefit.

Resources for OCD

OC Foundation, Inc.
PO Box 9573
New Haven, CT 06535-9573
(203) 315-2190

Obsessive-Compulsive Information Center
Madison Institute of Medicine
7617 Mineral Point Road
Suite 300
Madison, WI 53717
(608) 827-2470

National Institute of Mental Health
Public Inquiries
6001 Executive Blvd.
Room 8184 MSC 9663
Bethesda, MD 20892-9663
(301) 443-4513

Anxiety Disorders Association of America
8730 Georgia Avenue
Suite 600
Silver Spring, MD 20910
(240) 485-1001
web: www.adaa.org

Trichotillomania Learning Center
(Hair Pulling)
303 Potrero St.
Suite 51
Santa Cruz, CA 95060
(831) 457-1004

Hazelden Information and Educational Services
PO Box 176
15251 Pleasant Valley Road
Center City, MN 55012-0176
(800) 328-9000

Resources for Families

Co-dependents Anonymous
PO Box 33577 Phoenix, AZ 85067
(602) 277-7991

Emotions Anonymous
PO Box 4245, St. Paul, MN 55104
(651) 647-9712

It is our hope that independent OC-Anon support groups will form, using this book as needed for their program.

Footnotes

1. *Al-Anon Faces Alcoholism, 2nd Edition.* Al-Anon Family Group Headquarters Inc. New York 1992

2. ibid.

3. *Obsessive Compulsive Anonymous, Recovering from Obsessive Compulsive Disorder*, OCA, New Hyde Park, NY 1990

4. ibid.

5. *(Laundry List* for ACOA by Tony A. Health Communications, Deerfield Beach, FL.)

6. *OCA*

7. American Medical Association quoted in *Al-Anon Faces Alcoholism*

8. *OCA*

9. ibid.

10. Al-Anon

11. ibid.

New Second Edition

OBSESSIVE COMPULSIVE ANONYMOUS

Recovering From Obsessive Compulsive Disorder

We, of Obsessive Compulsive Anonymous (OCA), have all felt the fury of Obsessive Compulsive Disorder (OCD). OCD, with its crippling power, had left us physically, emotionally and spiritually sick.

Fortunately, the medical and psychological communities now have effective treatments for OCD. For many of us, though, this wasn't enough. The 12 Step Program of OCA has proven to be an important part in our continuing recovery from OCD.

ur book contains:

➢ The 12 Step Program for OCD
➢ Endorsements from psychiatrists and psychologists
➢ 33 of our personal stories of OCD
➢ How to start an OCA meeting
➢ Resources for OCD
➢ Slogans and tools we use

RECORDED LIVE

OCA 12 Step Workshop for OCD

Join longtime members of OCA as they guide the listener through our recovery program. If you are new to OCA or if your meeting is struggling with the question "How does the 12 Step program work for OCD,?" these audio cassettes will help! Recorded live at the Queens, New York meeting.

Please send the following:

❒ "*Obsessive Compulsive Anonymous Recovering from Obsessive Compulsive Disorder*" (2nd edition)
@ $19.00 per book* Sub total _____

❒ "*OCA – 12 Step Workshop for OCD*"
@ $35.00 per set of 4 cassette tapes* Sub total _____

*All prices include shipping and handling Total enclosed _____

Mail payment to:

OCA World Services
P.O. Box 215 • New Hyde Park, NY 11040• 516-739-0662
Please make check or money order payable to "OCA World Services" - U.S. Dollars/U.S. Bank

Name _____

Address _____

City / State / Zip _____

Additional Copies of: Obsessive Compulsive Disorder — A Survival Guide for Family and Friends can be obtained directly from the publisher.

Please send $10.00 per book in US dollars (check or money order U.S. Bank) to:

OCA World Services
PO Box 215
New Hyde Park, NY 11040

Shipping is included for US and Canadian delivery. Outside areas add actual shipping costs.

Mail to:

Name   _____

Address _____

City_____State_____Zip_____